James Bryan Smith

The KINGDOM
and the CROSS

IVP Books

An imprint of InterVarsity Press
Downers Grove, Illinois

D0048783

InterVarsity Press
P.O. Box 1400, Downers Grove, IL 60515-1426
World Wide Web: www.ivpress.com
E-mail: email@ivpress.com

InterVarsity Press® is the book-publishing division of InterVarsity Christian Fellowship/USA®, a movement of students and faculty active on campus at hundreds of universities, colleges and schools of nursing in the United States of America, and a member movement of the International Fellowship of Evangelical Students. For information about local and regional activities, write Public Relations Dept., InterVarsity Christian Fellowship/USA, 6400 Schroeder Rd., P.O. Box 7895, Madison, WI 53707-7895, or visit the IVCF website at <www.intervarsity.org>.

Scripture quotations, unless otherwise noted, are from the New Revised Standard Version of the Bible, copyright 1989 by the Division of Christian Education of the National Council of the Churches of Christ in the USA. Used by permission. All rights reserved.

Design: Cindy Kiple

Cover images: Jason Deines/iStockphoto

Interior images: Rublev's famous icon showing the three Angels being hosted by Abraham at Mambré: Alex Bakharev/Wikimedia Commons

                 Our Lady of Korsun: Testus/Wikimedia Commons

                 Michelangelo's Pieta: Stanislav Traykov/Wikimedia Commons

ISBN 978-0-8308-3549-2

Printed in the United States of America ∞

Library of Congress Cataloging-in-Publication Data

Smith, James Bryan.
   The Kingdom and the Cross / James Bryan Smith.
     p. cm.—(Apprentice resources)
   Includes bibliographical references (p.   ).
   ISBN 978-0-8308-3549-2 (pbk.: alk. paper)
   1. Christian life—Methodist authors. 2. Kingdom of God. 3. Holy Cross. I. Title.
   BV4501.3.S6524 2010
   248.4—dc22

                                            2010024963

P	21	20	19	18	17	16	15	14	13	12	11	10	9	8	7	6	5	4	3	2	1
Y	28	27	26	25	24	23	22	21	20	19	18	17	16	15	14	13	12	11	10		

formatio
TRADITION. EXPERIENCE.
TRANSFORMATION.

Formatio books from InterVarsity Press follow the rich tradition of the church in the journey of spiritual formation. These books are not merely about being informed, but about being transformed by Christ and conformed to his image. Formatio stands in InterVarsity Press's evangelical publishing tradition by integrating God's Word with spiritual practice and by prompting readers to move from inward change to outward witness. InterVarsity Press uses the chambered nautilus for Formatio, a symbol of spiritual formation because of its continual spiral journey outward as it moves from its center. We believe that each of us is made with a deep desire to be in God's presence. Formatio books help us to fulfill our deepest desires and to become our true selves in light of God's grace.

contents

introduction

$\int$o, what do you think?" is a question we are often asked. It may be about politics or global warming or handguns or prayer in schools. It may be about something someone has done or a project someone has run by you. People want to know what we think. I think this is good, because what we think is crucial. We live at the mercy of our ideas. What we think about things determines our actions.

While politics and projects are important, there are more important things for which our ideas and images play an even greater role. For example, what we think about God—the nature of God, God's character—is, I believe, the most important thing about us. How we answer that will determine our spiritual future, as well as how we live day by day. Jesus came to reveal the character of God and to reconcile the world. Two key concepts of the Christian faith are these: the kingdom of God and the cross. Jesus spoke over one hundred times about the kingdom, far more than any other subject. Surprisingly, we hear very little about the kingdom in our churches.

The kingdom is a life lived under the care, rule and provision of God, and it is entered by surrender. The cross was the greatest act in all of history, God dying to reconcile the world to himself. The cross is the most recognized symbol in the world.

So, what do you think about the kingdom? What do you think really happened on the cross? This little guide is meant to help expand your understanding of these two key concepts. I do not proclaim to have every answer about these subjects, nor do I assert that I have the best explanation of them. What I offer in this book are some of the ideas and images that have been helpful to me in my journey.

SOUL TRAINING

In addition to ideas, each chapter contains a soul training exercise. For those who have read other books in the Apprentice series, this will be very familiar to you. As a way of helping to embed the ideas and images in each chapter, I offer an exercise or activity that will help make the concepts clearer, and hopefully they will become more a part of our way of seeing and living. I must say, however, that the exercises in this guide are very different than the others in the Apprentice series. Here I wanted to focus a little more on using the "right side of the brain," so to speak.

Many of the exercises involve art, the use of icons and watching films. I believe that art is a great medium of communication, but I realize this is not true for everyone. A friend who is an engineer said of these kinds of exercises, "I get very little out of this stuff. My mind is analytical. I like to read and think about ideas. Looking at pictures and icons is not my cup of tea." While that is true for some, I believe that we can gain a lot from art, icons and movies, so I offer them as new ways for people to find out what they think about God, the kingdom and the cross.

Some Christians feel that icons, art and film border on idolatry (or maybe even *are* idolatrous). Catholics and Orthodox Christians are very comfortable with these mediums, but some Protestants have been raised to think that these activities are not only unhelpful but very dangerous. I understand that position, and I am wary of anyone who has reverence for an icon, a statue or a piece of art. Icons and art are at best *windows* to God. Windows are not for looking at but looking through. For me, icons and art are expressions of the character of God. They are theology in lines and colors. Still, if these things are hard for you to engage in, by all means do not do something that is uncomfortable for you.

READING IN COMMUNITY

At the end of the book is a group guide designed to help you and others to engage the ideas of the book and to share what you experienced in the exercises. This might be helpful to people or groups looking for resources to use during Lent. It can be used by an individual but is much more helpful when used in the context of a small group.

The concepts and ideas in this guide have been instrumental in helping me understand the nature of God, the kingdom and the cross. I hope in some way it will be helpful to you, and if you are in a group, to those who journey through it with you.

one

The Economy of the Kingdom

*Seek first his kingdom and his righteousness,
and all these things will be yours as well.*

MATTHEW 6:33 NIV

I was riding in a car with Dallas Willard somewhere between Colorado Springs and Denver. At one point I said, "Hey, could I get your advice on something?" He said sure.

I told him the following story: "Three years ago I invited a young man to speak at our chapel service. About the time I expected him to arrive he called me from a nearby town and told me his car had broken down. So I drove out to meet him and helped him get his car to a repair shop. The next day he spoke in chapel, and then I drove him to get his car. He spoke to the mechanic, who told him it was done, and then presented him with a bill. The young man came to me and said, 'Um, I am really embarrassed, but I don't have enough money to pay the bill. In fact, I don't have any money at all. Could you loan me the money, and I will pay you back in a week or so?'

"So I said I would. The bill turned out to be $400. I called my wife to let her know what I was doing, and she thought it was a good thing to do, helping someone out and all. So I paid the bill, and he took off for home. Several weeks passed and I never heard from him. Several weeks turned into several months, and still I heard nothing. Then, about a year later he left a message at work that said, 'Hey, I am really sorry, things are still really tight for me, but I want you to know that I haven't forgotten about the money I owe you. I should have it in a few weeks.' Once again, a few weeks turned into months, and now, two years later, I still have heard nothing from him. I am just wondering if it would all right if I called him, and if so, what should I say. What do you think, Dallas?"

Dallas paused, then looked at me and asked, "Have you missed it?"

I replied, "Have I missed . . . what?"

He explained, "Have you missed the money? Have you been living in a condition of need?"

I thought about it for a moment, and it occurred to me that over the past three years we had had adequate—actually more than adequate—provision for the things we need. I began to remember several instances when some large, unexpected bill (roof repair, new dishwasher, broken water pump in the car) had come along, and it was almost as if every time there was also some unexpected surplus that allowed us to survive unscathed. I remembered one time when we got an unexpected $500 bill for our daughter's medical care, and I didn't sleep well that night. Then, in the next day's mail we got a check from an anonymous source. The enclosed note said, "I really felt that God wanted me to send you this check. I have been praying for you and your daughter."

The check was for $500.

"No," I answered Dallas, "we have not missed it. We have been well cared for."

"You see, Jim," Dallas explained, "it is all about kingdom economics." I had heard of supply-side economics and voodoo economics, but never "kingdom" economics.

Dallas went on, "The kingdom of God is God's rule and reign, and when you surrendered your life to God you entered that kingdom. The essence of the Trinity is self-sacrifice. God is in the business of giving to others. When you gave your money freely to that man, you were aligned with God and his kingdom. God would then make sure that that money, given in sacrifice, would never be missed."

Something shifted in me during that car ride that has left me unalterably changed. Dallas pointed out something going on all around me that I failed to notice. God was with me. God had been watching over me. It was as if Dallas were Sherlock Holmes, who in the final scene points out fifteen clues that have been there all along but no one was paying attention to—except Holmes. When I added up all of the clues, it became clear that God had been very near my family and our needs. Kingdom economics is not a "get rich" scheme, but rather a system of providing for people's needs as they need it.

But more important than awakening me to the presence of the kingdom was the way it made me think about the King. What kind of God would care so much for me that something as trifling as my little financial bills matter to him? I began to suspect that God was out for my good, and if so, then he must be the kind of God who is indeed good. I had been learning that God is my Abba Father, that God is trustworthy and loving. Now I was coming into contact with a God who is utterly self-sacrificing.

Have you ever thought of God as "self-sacrificing"?

The key to what Dallas said was this: "The essence of the Trinity is self-sacrifice." That is an idea that is seldom talked about.

Many people view God as an angry judge who punishes us for our infractions. But the Christian story reveals a God who sacrifices for his creation out of sheer love. The incarnation—God becoming human—as well as the crucifixion—God dying for the human race—are indisputable evidence that the essence of God is love (1 John 4:8).

The Sermon on the Mount is, in my view, the greatest sermon ever given. And the central idea in that sermon comes in Matthew 6:33: "But strive first for the kingdom of God and his righteousness, and all these things will be given to you as well." The kingdom of God is found wherever God rules and reigns. We pray, "Thy kingdom come, thy will be done" in the Lord's Prayer. When we put the kingdom of God—an interactive life of surrender—at the center, everything we need will be provided for us. That is the essential promise of kingdom economics.

This week think about the utter gratuity of your life. You came into being out of grace. Though you may have faced hardship in your life, every day the sun came up and there was air to breath—all a gift. Your and my salvation are true acts of grace—we did nothing to deserve it. That is because God is giving. And as God's people, we take on his character and become giving people. Sometimes it takes a broken down car to teach us things like that.

Gazing on the Trinity Icon

Several years ago I became interested in icons, mainly through the writings of the Roman Catholic priest and spiritual writer Henri Nouwen. Henri is important to me in many ways. I once wrote him a letter about which seminary to attend. I ended up taking his advice— and am grateful I did. So when he wrote a little book about some icons that were meaningful in his spiritual life I was intrigued.

I know many people (mainly those who come from Protestant denominations) who have been taught to avoid placing any sacred worth in a material object, be it a picture or a statue. This is based on the commandment not to make any "graven images" of God (Exodus 20:4). Icons are neither "graven images" nor idols; rather, they are windows into the nature of God. Through colors and shapes and images an icon makes a theological statement; it tells the truth about God without using words. For me, reflecting on an icon is no different than reading a book about God, whether on theology or spirituality. But I am aware of the danger of turning an icon into an idol, treating it as if it were sacred in itself. What is sacred is not the wood or the paint, but the God it points to. That is why I think of icons as windows. We do not look *at* a window, we look *through* it.

In the book, Father Nouwen talks about one of the most famous icons of all time, the famous thirteenth-century icon of the Trinity by the Russian iconographer Rublev. It was originally painted onto a wall in a church in Russia. In this icon we see three "angels" in what appears to be a depiction of the Genesis 18 narrative about the angels who visit Abraham and Sarah to tell them they will give birth to a child in their old age. But Rublev was doing more than that. He was depicting the Trinity and telling us something important about God. The icon can be viewed in full color at http://commons.wikimedia.org/wiki/File:Angelsatmamre-trinity -rublev-1410.jpg.

On the right sits God the Father, with Jesus sitting at his right hand (the middle), and the Holy Spirit is on the left. The Father is

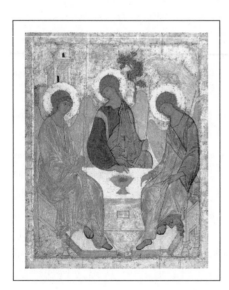

wearing gold to indicate he is the Creator. Jesus wears brown to indicate the earth, or his incarnation. And the Spirit wears green to indicate life, because the Spirit is the giver of life. (All three have some blue on to indicate heaven.) Notice how the Son and the Spirit are bowing toward the Father. This apparently indicates a kind of hierarchy in the Trinity. (Jesus said he only came to do the will of his Father, and the Spirit's role is to point us to the Father and the Son.)

But before we try to decide who is "boss," Rublev has the head of the Father equally bowed to the Son and Spirit. There is no hierarchy in the Trinity because the Trinity will not allow it; each of the members of the Trinity lives in constant submission and sacrifice to the others. Another aspect of the icon indicates equal authority in the Trinity: all three carry identical staffs (very thin lines, which are hard to see in a reproduction).

Notice also the right hand of Jesus. He is pointing with two fingers, which represent his humanity and divinity. He is fully God and fully human, an essential truth in Christianity. If he were less than God, he could not save the world, and if he were not truly human, he could not die, because God cannot die. Finally, notice the very center of the icon. Everything is pointing to the center of the table, where a chalice sits.

The chalice represents two things. First, it represents the "cup" Jesus chose to endure, namely, his suffering and self-sacrifice. Second, the cup represents the chalice used in Communion, the Eucharist or the Lord's Supper. When Christians gather to take Communion, they are remembering the sacrifice of Jesus. What Rublev teaches me when I gaze on this icon is that the Trinity is a community of love, submission and sacrifice.

This icon has helped me understand unity. All three members of the Trinity are huddled together, like three people working closely on a project. The project, in this case, is the reconciliation of the world. God the Father, God the Son and God the Spirit are in collusion. I picked up a false narrative early on that has been hard to shake, namely, that Jesus died on the cross to avert the wrath of God the Father. As if God the Father were simmering in anger and ready to destroy bad humans, but Jesus, the good Son, steps in to take our punishment. This narrative leaves me with a nice Jesus and a mean Father; it also creates a tension in the Trinity, as if they were at odds with each other. Rublev's depiction of the Trinity helps me see the true narrative, the one that is in keeping with the tenor of the Christian story. When I saw that God the Father was also making a sacrifice for us, it changed my view of the Father. Hopefully, it does something similar for you.

two

A God who seeks our Good

For surely I know the plans I have for you, says the LORD, plans for your welfare and not for harm, to give you a future with hope.

JEREMIAH 29:11

There are two common core narratives when it comes to God and God's provision. The first is commonly heard from more conservative Christians: "God blesses the righteous."

This core narrative is easy to defend from the Bible. We read in many places in the Bible about the blessings that will be reaped by the morally upright:

For you bless the righteous, O LORD;
you cover them with favor as with a shield. (Psalm 5:12)

This theme is prevalent in Scripture. It is a deeply entrenched core narrative in the minds of many, leading them to suspect that any good in their lives is a sign God is happy with them, and any trial they encounter is an indication they are being cursed.

While it is true that unique blessings are discovered only by the righteous (a functional soul, a quiet conscience), to say that God only blesses and cares for the righteous is indefensible. This false narrative was articulated very clearly to me one summer when I was working as a youth pastor in a small church. A very conservative religious group was attracting a small number of kids from our church. Many of the parents were concerned because this group required the kids to keep very strict rules concerning dress and behavior. So I agreed to meet with the two women leading this group. We sat down to talk, and after a few minutes I said, "Can we start by praying together?" One woman answered, "We already prayed before you came. We cannot pray with you. Jehovah only hears the prayers of the righteous."

This core narrative fails to fit with the Bible. The Bible is a veritable "Who's Who" of the *unrighteous*, those who have done nothing to merit God's kindness, whose prayers were heard by God and were subsequently helped by God. Adam and Eve led humanity into sin. Abraham cheats and lies, and Sarah laughs at God. Moses kills a man and displeases God many times. David has a man killed in order to possess the man's wife. Saul, soon to become the apostle Paul, hates Gentiles and wants to kill them.

It is almost as if being qualified, talented and skilled bars people from having God help them. I guess that is because when we are qualified, talented and skilled, it's likely we are not going to turn to God for help. We can manage on our own. And if we look at Alcoholics Anonymous, an organization that has helped multitudes attain transformed lives, we see that its first requirement is that people reach the point at which they can say, "We admitted

Have you been exposed to the idea that God only hears the prayers of those who are "righteous"? How did it effect your relationship with God?

we were powerless . . . that our lives had become unmanageable." This is a club that demands of its members not self-help but self-surrender.

So since God blesses not only the righteous, the upright and the pure (and who are these people, anyway, because I haven't met one yet?), and is not helping those who help themselves (but seems fond of helping those who cannot), then in terms of caring and provision and blessing, what kind of person does God take care of? Once again, we need to ask that question of Jesus. His core narratives always ring true.

Jesus reveals a God who is out for our good—all of us. Regardless of what we have done or how we have failed, God is doing anything and everything to reach us. God searches for us like a lost sheep or a lost coin; each day God eagerly awaits the return of his prodigal children. So few people—so few Christians—truly believe that God seeks their good. Many have been trained to think that God has been storing up his wrath and will one day unleash it. They may fear this God, but they cannot love this God. But the God that Jesus reveals is a God who always wants the best for us. And that is a God we cannot help but love.

Looking out for the Good of others

In the opening chapter I talked about how God, by nature, is self-giving. I told of a time I reluctantly gave money to help a person in need, and spent several years fretting about not getting repaid. But my friend Dallas Willard relieved me of my worry. He led to me to see that, in the economy of the kingdom, the things we give are never lost.

In this chapter I shifted the focus to another aspect of God, namely, that God seeks our good and longs to bless us even when we do not deserve it. One of the core narratives I live by is, As God is, so his people should become. Because Christ dwells in me, I am (or should be) reflecting more and more of the character of Christ in my life. So, if our God is self-sacrificing and seeks to bless others who have done nothing to merit it, then we should be people who are self-sacrificing and who bless others who have not earned it.

So, how do we do this? First, begin by asking God to bring you this week someone you can help in some way. (Be careful—these kinds of prayers always get answered!) Next, keep your eye out for who this might be. It could a friend, a coworker, a person you meet at the grocery store, or a family or couple who live in your neighborhood. Finally, ask permission to help. Keep in mind that being helped or served puts a person in a position of need, and that may be uncomfortable. (I know it is for me. To ask for or receive help makes me feel vulnerable.) So be sure to say, "May I help you?"

What kinds of things am I thinking about? Below are some examples of ways God has answered my prayer to help others by giving me a chance to act as he does:

1. Listening. This is a wonderful way to help someone. Just ask a friend or family member how they are doing, or how their life is going. And then listen.

2. Helping. Rarely does a day pass when I do not run across people who could use a little help with something. It may be as simple as holding a door or letting someone in your lane while driving. Or it may be as challenging as helping someone move or paint their home.

3. Letting others "win" arguments. I call this "letting others have the last word." In a discussion we sometimes feel the need to have the final say or to win the argument. This week let others have that last word, and simply respond, "You may be right." Many of my students find this exercise both challenging and rewarding.

three

The Grace of the Incarnation

*"Look, the virgin shall conceive and bear a son, and they shall
name him Emmanuel," which means, "God is with us."*

MATTHEW 1:23

God made a beautiful world. It is full of breathtaking sights,
sounds and smells. I was recently in the Rocky Mountains and
was in awe of their beauty. Honeysuckle is now blooming where I
live, and each morning I step outside to get the newspaper the
smell of the blooms is intoxicating. It is all an act of grace. I did
nothing to earn any of it. The beauty of God's grace is all around
me. But the most beautiful image of grace the world has ever
known is the incarnation: God becoming human.

The incarnation is God's self-giving act of freely choosing to enter our world in the person of Jesus. In so doing God took the en-
tirety of our condition on himself and experienced every aspect of
human life, including pain, doubt, suffering and loneliness. Whatever bad experience we may have encountered, we can be sure that

Jesus has also encountered it. Thomas Torrance explains:

> The Incarnation is to be understood as the coming of God to take upon himself our fallen human nature, our actual human existence laden with sin and guilt, our humanity diseased in mind and soul in its estrangement or alienation from the Creator. This is a doctrine found everywhere in the early Church in the first five centuries, expressed again and again in the terms that the whole man had to be assumed by Christ if the whole man was to be saved.

Jesus, then, was fully human. There is no aspect of being human that Jesus did not experience. Sometimes wealthy people spend a weekend among the poor as one of them. While this beneficial exercise helps people experience what it is like to be poor and perhaps increases their compassion, the truth is that these wealthy people do not truly experience what it means to be poor. Why? Because they are not poor. At any moment they can walk away from it. They don't know what it means to be poor, to not know whether they are going to eat tonight or have a place to sleep or be able to get help if they become ill.

Some people think of Jesus and the incarnation this way. They believe that he was just God hiding inside a human suit, like Clark Kent trying to keep his Superman status clandestine. At any moment Clark can fly or stop a bullet. He is not fully human. He does not know what it is like to be human, to be weak and vulnerable. Maybe that is why the author introduced kryptonite. It is not a compelling story if the hero has no weakness. But Jesus is not like Superman. He became fully human. And that is the compelling part of the story.

EXPERIENCING HUMAN LIFE
Why did Jesus have to experience every aspect of human life?

As Torrance notes, quoting the fourth-century church father Athanasius, "That which is not assumed cannot be healed." Meaning, if there were some part of life (say, doubt) that Jesus was not capable of, then he could not redeem that part of life. As we read in Hebrews, "For we do not have a high priest who is unable to sympathize with our weaknesses, but we have one who in every respect has been tested as we are, yet without sin" (Hebrews 4:15).

But he does sympathize with our weaknesses. Jesus cried, doubted, suffered, watched friends die, knew betrayal and underwent as much physical pain as a body can take and still live, and with what strength he had left he willingly carried his cross to his own execution. And then he experienced the absolute worst thing: he cried out from the cross, "Why have you forsaken me?" The beloved Son, in whom God was well pleased, felt utter alienation and forsakenness. Is there anything worse?

All of this was necessary. "But why?" some have asked me, "Why would God will this to happen? What kind of God would set up this kind of arrangement?" The answer reveals something about the very nature and essence of God. But let's explore the other options first. Why did God have to do it this way? Why didn't God just show up on a giant TV screen in the sky and say to the people, "Hey, I really love you guys. And I am going to forgive the sin thing. So from now on, you are forgiven. OK? I am not mad anymore. Call me when you need me." We could have avoided the whole whipping, beating and crucifixion part.

Have you ever wondered if there could have been another way for God to save the world than to die on the cross? What questions do you have about crucifixion?

We are fond of this approach because we like power. And we are uncomfortable with God's approach because we are not fond of self-sacrifice. Had God declared forgiveness by divine fiat, as I suggested, some "clearing the decks" with a pronouncement from on high, he would not have been involved in our salvation, restoration and healing. Here is the key: *by nature God is self-giving.* Edward Yarnold's explanation is profound:

> Why did the Father will [the crucifixion]? . . . May one suggest that the answer is that human nature is made in God's own image? The law of the grain of wheat reflects God's own nature: the glory of God himself lies in self-giving. The members' of Christ's body, then, share the life of the Head, who bears a crown of glory which is still a crown of thorns.

At the heart of the universe is this one principle: self-sacrifice is the highest act. The grain of wheat must die in order to give life. The cosmos reflects the nature of the God who created it.

What does the cross mean to you?

God the Son enters our world in the lowest of all conditions, lives an utterly ordinary life for thirty years so that he might experience everything we experience, points the world to his Father in his teaching and in his life, and then willingly (though not without doubt, confusion and anguish) performs the ultimate sacrifice: he gives his life for all of the world; the Lamb of God takes away the sin of the world.

"I will sacrifice myself for your good" is the sentiment of God. And we, in our small moments of sacrifice, feel something of what God feels (freedom, release, exhilaration, purpose, meaning), if only for a few moments. Jesus is called Emmanuel, which means "God with us." The kingdom of God is life with God. Jesus lived with God, but more than that, Jesus *is* life with God. When we surrender to Jesus, the one who lived in surrender to God, we enter into the kingdom of God. We did not earn it. It is an act of grace, built on the self-sacrifice of God.

Gazing on the cheek-to-cheek icon

An icon that has become meaningful to me is an icon of Mary and Jesus, sometimes called the cheek-to-cheek icon because Jesus and his mother are embracing one another by touching each other's face. There are several basic forms of icons, such as the one where Jesus is by himself, holding the Bible in his left hand, which is known as "Christ the Pantocrator." You will see many variations of the basic styles of icons, but I like the "cheek-to-cheek" icon because of the many things it teaches me. You can view the icon in color on the web at http://commons.wikimedia.org/wiki/File:Our_Lady_of_Korsun.jpeg.

What does this icon teach us? I see in it tenderness and sorrow. Mary's eyes are somewhat sad, and yet there great love between mother and child. I see the humanity of Jesus in the love he has for his mother. There is a lot to notice, but the one thing I always see, the main thing I am drawn to is Mary's hand. Her right hand is in a gesture of invitation or welcome, as if she is motioning to us, "Come and join in our love. It is a love filled with sorrow, but it is a strong love that can never be broken."

The incarnation is a thing of wonder. The mighty God becomes a tiny baby. The invincible, all-powerful God needs to be burped and fed. But as we have seen, God often seems paradoxical because love is paradoxical. Love loves the unlovely. Power is made

perfect in weakness. The last will be first. A person has to die to
live. And the great paradox in this icon is that love invites us,
Mary's hand invites us, even though we do not deserve it. Love
loves without condition.

I have this icon next to the Rublev Trinity icon on the wall of
the room where I pray. I like to look at the Trinity icon, reflecting

on the preexistent Jesus, the
Logos, who lived in community with the Father and the
Spirit long before the world
was made. As they sit at table
the Trinity conspires to save
humanity. Then I turn my
attention to the cheek-to-
cheek icon, reflecting on the
incredible idea that God
willingly allowed himself to
enter our world as a baby. Jesus, who made the universe,
including the angels, allows
himself to become utterly
helpless. Human babies are among the most helpless of all off-
spring. For at least a few years a human child relies completely on
a parent or caregiver to survive.

The King of kings and Lord of lords chose to become one of the
most helpless creatures in the world. When I gaze on the Trinity
icon, I reflect on the power of God; when I gave upon the cheek-
to-cheek icon, I reflect on the powerlessness of God. What could
have made God do this? Why would Jesus subject himself to this
indignity? There is only one reason—the nature of God is love.

four

god emptied himself

The Word became flesh and lived among us.

JOHN 1:14

I once spoke at a conference based on the Apprentice series of books, and I was the main speaker. I sat down at a table near the front of the hall about fifteen minutes before my opening talk was to begin. The only person at my table was a lovely older lady. She did not have any idea I was the speaker. She held up a copy of the book *The Good and Beautiful God*, which I wrote, and asked, "Have you read this book?" I said, "Yes, I have." She said, "Well, it looks pretty good so far. I hope it is. And I hope this conference is good. My pastor encouraged me to come." I said, "I hope it is as well."

We went on to have a nice conversation and made a lot of connections. She was about the same age my mother would have been (my mother had passed years earlier) and grew up the same town as my mother. I imagined that they probably had seen each other at some point. It was so nice to hear about her life and her faith.

Then the host of the conference got up, read a very glowing intro-
duction of the main speaker, and said, "Let's give a nice welcome
to our speaker for tonight and tomorrow, James Bryan Smith." At
that point I stood up and walked to the podium. I looked back at
the lady at my table, and she had a look of both astonishment and
embarrassment.

During a break I sat down, and she said, "I am so embarrassed. I
sat talking to you like you were just a regular person attending this
conference. I had no idea you were famous and important." Though
she felt embarrassed, her words (albeit said in kindness) actually
embarrassed me. I was exactly the same person before and after my
opening talk. She acted like I had become someone else, someone
"famous and important." It hit me just how much we pay homage to
people who are famous in some way. I have never been comfortable
thinking of myself as more important than someone else. Frankly,
I enjoyed our conversation more before she knew I was the author
of the book. *Maybe,* I thought to myself, *Jesus assumed such a lowly
condition when he was born and raised because he wanted to connect
with people, not merely to impress them.*

The Word (or Logos in the original Greek) refers to Jesus. John
tells us he was with God in before all of creation, that Christ was
with God, and that he is God. We also learn from this passage that
the Word created the world, or was God's agent of creation, and
that "without him not one thing came into being." The word *Logos*
speaks volumes about the sacrificial nature of God.

LOGOS

In chapter three we looked at the sheer wonder of the incarnation.
The stunning aspect of the incarnation is this: "And the Word
became flesh and lived among us." So imagine it this way: Jesus is
God (the only begotten Son) who exists before all worlds, and
who, by his work, creates the universe. Jesus is not only present at

the moment of creation, he brings it into being—he makes galaxies and black holes and quarks and planets and oceans and whales and trees and monkeys and raspberries. And then one day the one who stood outside of time steps into time and decides to become a human—a zygote, an embryo, a fetus and then an infant.

The God who made air is now dependent on air to survive. The God who made humans must now depend on two humans (Mary and Joseph) to feed and care for him.

Why would God do this? Why the dramatic downward move? Because it is God's nature to love. God is love, and love wills the good of another, and that usually involves self-sacrifice. Philippians 2:6-11 is a beautiful, lyrical description of the wonder of the incarnation. Some scholars think it might have been an early Christian hymn; others think Paul composed and often recited it. Either way, it captures the essence of what it was like for Jesus to "empty" himself of his power and greatness, in order to rescue the fallen, broken world.

> What feelings arise when you picture what it would be like for God to enter our universe?

> Though he was in the form of God,
>   did not regard equality with God
>   as something to be exploited,
> *but emptied himself,*
>   taking the form of a slave,
>   being born in human likeness.
> And being found in human form,
>   he humbled himself
> and became obedient to the point of death—
>   even death on a cross.
>
> Therefore God also highly exalted him

and gave him the name
that is above every name,
so that at the name of Jesus
every knee should bend,
in heaven and on earth and under the earth,
and every tongue should confess
that Jesus Christ is Lord,
to the glory of God the Father.
(Philippians 2:6-11, italics added)

KENOSIS

The word *emptied* (v. 7) comes from the Greek word *kenosis*. Kenosis means to nullify, or make ineffectual. Jesus was God, equal with God, but chose to empty himself of his power and authority as God, taking on the humble form of a human. He was unlimited in power as the second member of the Trinity; he became limited, finite and able to die as the Son of Man. Still, he could have been born into a power family of noble bearing. Yet he did not come as a mighty warrior or a wealthy king. He comes in the humblest of conditions. And Jesus takes one more step: he willingly becomes obedient to death on the cross, perhaps history's cruelest form of execution. God empties himself. God sacrifices himself, because God's design is to draw all people to him.

How could God willingly do such a thing? Love is the only motive strong enough to produce this kind of sacrifice.

In nearly all of the world's religions—and certainly the earliest, primitive religions—sacrifice involves a human action (offering animals, flowers, fruit, obedient living) in order to insure that the god(s) will act favorably toward a person or group. Christianity, in contrast, is the only religion in which God makes a sacrifice in order to elevate humans.

The crucifixion was not a weak moment or a half-baked idea on God's part. Self-sacrifice is the very nature of God. And for those who live with God in his kingdom, the cross becomes a way of life or, more clearly, the way *to* life. This is the great paradox of the Christian faith.

watching *The Passion of the Christ*

The spiritual tool I would like you to practice this week is to meditate on the suffering and death of Jesus. I know this may seem morbid to some, but this practice has a long history, and done rightly, it will make a significant mark on your soul.

In his book *The Divine Conspiracy,* Dallas Willard writes, "The key, then, to loving God is to see Jesus, to hold him before the mind with as much fullness and clarity as possible. It is to adore him." He goes on to say that when we meditate on the passion, suffering and death of Jesus we are moved to this thought: "I am bought by the sufferings and death of Jesus and I belong to God. The divine conspiracy of which I am a part stands over human history in the form of a cross."

Dallas continues:

The individual disciples [apprentices of Jesus] must have indelibly imprinted upon their souls the reality of this wonderful person who walked among us and suffered a cruel death to enable each of us to have life in God. It should become something that is never beyond the margins of their consciousness. . . . No one can have an adequate view of the heart and purposes of the God of the universe who does not understand that he permitted his son to die on the cross to reach out to all people, even people who hated him. That is who God is. . . . It is God looking at me from the cross with compassion and providing for me, with never-failing readiness to take my hand to walk on through life from wherever I may find myself at the time."

Each year, on Good Friday, I watch the movie *The Passion of the Christ*. I do so because I want to remember the sacrifice Jesus made not only for me but for the world. The film does a beautiful job of showing the humanness of Jesus, particularly in his relationship with his mother. This week, if you are able, I encourage you to view this film. (I realize that the film is excessively violent, so I recommend this only for those who are mature enough to separate art from reality.) As you do, reflect on the meaning of the suffering of Jesus. Think about the willingness of God to die for us. If you like, repeat this phrase from Dallas as you meditate on these two images: "I am bought by the sufferings and death of Jesus and I belong to God. The divine conspiracy of which I am a part stands over human history in the form of a cross."

You may want to write down your reflections immediately after you view the film.

five

NO Greater Love

No one has greater love than this,
to lay down one's life for one's friends.

JOHN 15:13

Several years ago my brother experienced kidney failure and needed a donor kidney. The best donor matches are family members who share the same blood type. Naturally, I was asked to consider giving him one of my kidneys, though he was kind enough not to make me feel obligated. I told him I would do it. Then the scary facts were given: the operation could be damaging and is sometimes (though rarely) fatal. I was faced with the prospect of dying on the operating table while trying to offer my brother a good kidney, which would help him for the next ten to twenty years. Even if everything went perfectly, I would go the rest of my life with one kidney, not two, and while that is not life-threatening, it is certainly a sacrifice.

Part of me felt certain that it was the right decision. On the other hand, I had a wife and two small children, and I felt a lot of responsibility to take care of them. What would happen if I died?

A week later I went in for testing, and it turned out my brother and I have different blood types, which made my kidney a very bad match. He would be better off with a cadaver donor kidney as long as it matched his blood type. Within a year he found exactly that, and within time his health returned. We found out the donor's age and his occupation, but little else. I was thankful for this man and for the fact that he had signed the organ-donor release form at one time in his life.

Have you ever been asked to make a great sacrifice for another? If so, describe that experience. If not, how do you think you would react to the kind of sacrifice the author was asked to make?

That experience made me reflect a lot on the nature of sacrifice. We hear stories of people who die in order to save others. Just the other day I read a story about a man who jumped into a raging river to save a young boy—which he did—only to be swept up by the water, and in saving another he lost his own life. I was faced with far less: my brother was not going to die (he could have stayed on dialysis for many years) and neither was I (at least there was very little chance I would). Still, I was asked, for the first time in my life, to consider doing something utterly selfless in order to help another.

In a strange way I gained a new appreciation for the sacrifice of Jesus. His words "No one has greater love than this, to lay down one's life for one's friends" meant a little more to me. As I said, we cannot compare organ donation (or bone marrow donation), as noble as it is, to offering our life for the life of another. I made me realize how shallow my own love can be, and how great God's love for us is. I related to Peter, who at one point blurted out that he would give his life for Jesus, but Jesus, being wise, knew Peter's limitations:

Peter said to him, "Lord, why can I not follow you now? I will lay down my life for you." Jesus answered, "Will you lay down your life for me? Very truly, I tell you, before the cock crows, you will have denied me three times." (John 13:37-38)

In our better moments we assume that we would give our lives for those we love. I am sure Peter meant it when he said he would lay down his life for Jesus. The problem was not in Peter's intention; it was in his soul. When things finally turned dark for Jesus, when it looked as if the whole ministry project was doomed, Peter found himself fulfilling Jesus' prophecy: before Thursday night ended, he had denied Jesus three times.

I am like Peter. I am one part hero and nine parts chicken. I have moments of self-sacrifice but days of self-centeredness. I suspect I am not alone. The good news is that you and I are not Jesus. We are not called to save the world, even though we act like it sometimes. The very good news is that Jesus died for us. He did for us what we could never do for ourselves. As God, he willingly chose to die, and that death is proof of his love for us. For that reason, the following are two of my favorite verses:

But God proves his love for us in that while we were still sinners Christ died for us. (Romans 5:8)

In this is love, not that we loved God but that he loved us and sent his Son to be the atoning sacrifice for our sins. (1 John 4:10)

Later John proclaims, "We love because he first loved us" (1 John 4:19). God's love, demonstrated on the cross, establishes that we are loved. The only natural response is to love God in return.

Gazing on the *Pieta*

For several summers I assisted Dallas Willard in a course he taught for Fuller Seminary. We held this course at the Mater Dolorosa monastery, which means "Mother of sorrows." It is run by the Passionist Fathers, a Roman Catholic order that stresses meditating on the suffering of Jesus. Throughout the monastery there are several life-size and lifelike crucifixes. These priests and monks believe that as they meditate on the suffering and death of Jesus, they deepen their love for him.

How does this work, exactly? How can gazing on an image of Jesus on the cross, for example, affect our soul? Dallas notes that when we gaze on our crucified Lord we "bring the heart-wrenching goodness of God, his incomprehensible graciousness and generosity" before our minds. Dallas concludes, "The key, then, to loving God is to see Jesus." And to see or meditate on the broken and lifeless body of Jesus is to witness the pinnacle of his sacrificial nature.

This week I would like to invite you to engage fully with one of the most famous pieces of art ever created. It is a famous sculpture by Michelangelo, called the *Pieta*. It depicts Jesus on his mother's lap after he has been taken down from the cross. Michelangelo captures a moment of absolute sorrow in this sculpture. The artist was commissioned to create this work of art from a single slab of marble when he was only twenty-eight years old. The power of the sculpture catapulted Michelangelo to fame and the creation of his

masterpiece, the ceiling of the Sistine Chapel. He used the arts to move the hearts of people, to help them love and appreciate the sacrifice of God. You can view this sculpture on the web at http://commons.wikimedia .org/wiki/File:Michelangelo %27s_Pieta_5450.jpg.

Holding an image before your mind is a powerful tool to help deepen your devotion to God. When I look at the *Pieta* I am reminded by the words of Jesus: "No one has greater love than this, to lay down one's life for one's friends." When I look at the *Pieta* I am moved by the love of God. Jesus did not merely die for the good people. He died for sinners (Romans 5:8), which is you and me, people who sometimes get it together but mostly struggle to remain faithful and obedient.

I am also struck by the way the artist depicts the face of Mary. In the cheek-to-cheek icon (see p. 26) Mary looks very grieved. When Simeon blessed the baby Jesus in the temple, he added a word to Mary:

Then Simeon blessed them and said to his mother Mary, "This child is destined for the falling and the rising of many in Israel, and to be a sign that will be opposed so that the inner thoughts of many will be revealed—and a sword will pierce your own soul too. (Luke 2:34-35)

From his birth Mary knew the destiny of her son. In the cheek-to-cheek icon you see her deep sorrow. But in the *Pieta*, Michelangelo wanted to convey something different. He wanted to show the serenity of Mary. Jesus completed his mission, and though her heart is broken she has come to accept his death. She had many years to prepare. And, after all, she was the one who said from the beginning, "Let it be with me according to your word" (Luke 1:38).

I get so much from the photo I have of this statue. It sits on my desk, and I see it every day. I want to practice what Dallas said: the key to loving God is to see Jesus. When I look at the *Pieta*, when I reflect on our God who died for us or think about the journey of Mary, I find myself loving God even more.

SIX

The Deeper Magic

For in him all the fullness of God was pleased to dwell, and through him God was pleased to reconcile to himself all things, whether on earth or in heaven, by making peace through the blood of his cross.

Colossians 1:19-20

There are a lot of theories of the atonement, which try to explain what Jesus accomplished on the cross. One popular theory is the *forensic* theory: Jesus took the punishment we deserve on himself so that we do not have to suffer. It is like a courtroom in which each of us stand before the Judge (God the Father), are found guilty and are sentenced to die. Then Jesus stands before the bench and asks to die in our place. The Judge allows it, and we are set free.

This theory is very popular and can be heard in many sermons each week. It explains an important dimension of what Jesus did for us.

Another theory of the atonement known as *Christus Victor* focuses in the victory of Jesus. This theory emphasizes how Jesus defeated the two great foes of the human race: sin and death. Jesus lived a sinless life; he kept the law perfectly. He reversed the curse of the law, which is the precursor to sin. And by rising from the grave Jesus defeated death. So those who believe in him reign with him over sin, having been reconciled by his blood, and they also have no fear of death, for Jesus has soundly defeated it.

Those are just two theories of how Jesus' death atones for our sin and brings us to God. But the earliest theory of the atonement is sometimes referred to as the fishhook theory. It dates back to the early centuries of the church. In this explanation Jesus baited a hook and tempted Satan with it, and Satan took it. Humanity deserved to die for their waywardness and sin, and subsequently lived under the dominion of the prince of this world, Satan. Jesus, this theory proposes, went to Satan and said, "Let the people be free. Take me instead." Satan hates the human race because we are God's creation and the apple of God's eye. But because God is Satan's great enemy, the chance to take God down through God's Son could not be resisted. Satan agreed to the bargain, and Jesus offered himself to Satan. As Jesus hung on the cross, Satan was sure he had won.

Which theory of the atonement did you hear the most when you were growing up? How did it effect your view of God?

We see the fishhook theory in C. S. Lewis's classic *The Lion, the Witch, and the Wardrobe*. Lewis has Aslan, the great lion who is the Christ figure, tricking the White Witch (Satan) by offering himself to pay the price of Edmund's transgression. But the White Witch does not know "the deeper magic," namely, that an innocent one who dies willingly for the sake of another creates a force of energy more powerful than death. Aslan is mocked, beaten and killed, and the White Witch assumes she has obtained total control over Narnia. But Aslan rises from the dead, and soon the

Witch and all her forces are overtaken. Though Aslan is struck down, he rises more powerful than before.

Even the *Star Wars* films, which are a syncretistic blending of many religious ideas and images, contains at the heart the idea that self-preservation is destructive, and self-sacrifice is the highest power. When Obi Wan Kenobi battles Darth Vadar with light sabers, before he voluntarily surrenders, he says, "If you strike me down, I will become more powerful than you can imagine." We hear echoes of Christian theology in that story. Jesus was struck down willingly, and became more powerful than we can imagine.

"Deeper magic" is at the core of Christianity. In a world of power, force and violence, the notion of humility and self-sacrifice are hard to imagine. But love is indeed more powerful than hate. God reconciled the whole world to himself not by divine fiat but by laying down his life. Jesus not only reconciled the world to God, he also defeated death. On the third day, he rose from the grave.

The fishhook theory is interesting to me because it was a favorite of the early church, and also because it is one we seldom hear. I do not think it is the best theory of the atonement. I am not sure there is a *best* theory. I get so much out of all of them: the forensic, courtroom theory helps me see my sin, and Jesus' willingness to die for me helps me feel grateful for his sacrifice; the Christus Victor explanation gives me hope and courage through the undeniable victory of our Lord over sin and death. However, I offer the fishhook theory simply because most of the Christians I know have never heard of it (until I mention Lewis's book or the movie). I also offer it because it helps us see that the source of sacrifice is love, which is the deeper magic.

EASTER TRIUMPH

No greater love has the world seen than the cross. But the great mystery of the world is this: God's power is made perfect in weakness (2 Corinthians 12:9). On the third day Jesus rose from the dead. He defeated death. Christ the Victim is now Christ the Victor. Christ endured the cross and now wears the crown. Self-sacrifice is not weakness. The courage to lay down our life for another is the greatest power this world has ever known. The empty tomb validates the truth that good triumphs over evil.

Things looked dark on that Friday we call "Good." But God gets the last word: "And I, when I am lifted up from the earth, will draw all people to myself" (John 12:32).

watching *The Lion, the Witch, and the Wardrobe*

I would like to recommend another film for you to watch as a soul-shaping exercise. The film *The Lion, the Witch, and the Wardrobe* is an excellent adaption of C. S. Lewis's children's novel by the same title. It captures the adventure and the wonder of the Christian story, and it allows children and adults to enter into the great mystery of redemption. In this allegory of the Christian faith, Aslan, the great lion, is a Christ figure. He is all-powerful, but he willingly offers his life in exchange for the boy Edmund, whose betrayal of his family warrants death.

The White Witch is a Satan figure bent on taking over the world through force, deception and cruelty. Even sin is depicted by Lewis as the irresistible candy Turkish Delight, which Edmund betrayed his family in order to have. Of course, Lewis's allegory is simply that: an allegory. It is not a complete view of the atonement. Lewis himself described the atonement in other ways in his other works, both fiction and nonfiction. The fishhook theory is simply one narrative people have used to explain the glorious and mysterious act of love we call the cross. That is what is so great about art. It can help us see another aspect of beauty and truth that we did not see before.

Rent or buy a copy of this great film and think about the "deeper magic" and the deep message it offers.

Appendix

Small Group Discussion Guide

This discussion guide is designed to help a group of friends, small group or Sunday school class to experience the book together. A group can range from two to twelve people. Each session is split into multiple segments. Use these segments in whatever way is comfortable in your setting. You may want to skip some and expand others. The sessions are designed to take about 45 minutes.

CHAPTER 1: THE ECONOMY OF THE KINGDOM

OPENING TO GOD [5 MINUTES]
Begin with five minutes of silence followed by a brief prayer inviting God to guide the conversation. Why five minutes of silence?

We live in a world that is filled with noise and distractions. It is easy to enter one conversation still processing the last conversation. In the midst of all this busyness it is also difficult to hear the whispering voice of God. When we gather with friends to share our spiritual journey, we want to hear God's voice in the lives of those around us. With a little silence we will be prepared to listen; so one option is to begin each gathering with some silence.

SOUL TRAINING: GAZING ON THE TRINITY ICON [10-15 MINUTES]

If you are in a group of seven or more people, divide into small groups of three or four. Spend ten minutes discussing what the soul-training experience was like.

ENGAGING THE CHAPTER [10-15 MINUTES]

1. Have you ever had a situation like the author's, where someone borrowed something from you (money, tools, books) and did not return it? How did you deal with it?

2. Have you ever thought of God as self-sacrificing?

3. The author writes, "as God's people, we take on his character and become giving people." How would you rate yourself as a giving person?

ENGAGING THE WORD [10-20 MINUTES]

The central text for this chapter is Matthew 6:33:

Seek first his kingdom and his righteousness, and all these things will be yours as well. (NIV)

As an individual or a group, read the passage aloud three times. Each time you read it or hear it read, pay attention to which words or phrases stand out to you. It may change between the first and third reading. Either circle those words or phrases or write them down on a separate page. After you have determined which word or words seemed to resonate with you, ask the Holy Spirit to help you see any special connection those words might have for you. (Pray like this: "What are you trying to teach me, Lord?") Listen. Write down anything that comes to you. This is an ancient practice called *lectio divina.*

After you have finished this exercise personally, allow time for everyone in the group to share whatever word or insight they have discovered, if they feel comfortable. This exercise can lead to very personal insights and discoveries that you may not yet feel ready to share with others.

GO IN PEACE [5 MINUTES]
Pray the Lord's Prayer together out loud.

CHAPTER 2: A GOD WHO SEEKS OUR GOOD

OPENING TO GOD [5 MINUTES]
Begin with five minutes of silence followed by a brief prayer inviting God to guide the conversation.

SOUL TRAINING: LOOKING OUT FOR THE GOOD OF OTHERS [10-15 MINUTES]
If you are in a group of seven or more people, divide into small groups of three or four. Spend ten minutes discussing what the soul-training experience was like.

ENGAGING THE CHAPTER [10-15 MINUTES]
1. The author tells the story of when two women from another religious group said they were right and he was wrong. Have

you ever had an experience like that? If so, describe it.

2. Have you been exposed to the idea that God only hears the prayers of those who are "righteous"? Did it influence how you related to God?

3. The author writes, "Many have been trained to think that God has been storing up his wrath and will one day unleash it. They may fear this God, but they cannot love this God." If you had to rate how much you truly love God on a scale of 1-10 (10 being the highest), what number would you give? What could you do, according to this chapter, to improve that score?

ENGAGING THE WORD [10-20 MINUTES]
Lectio divina (see the directions in this group guide for chap. 1)
This week's passage:

Surely I know the plans I have for you, says the Lord, plans for your welfare and not for harm, to give you a future with hope. (Jeremiah 29:11)

After you have finished this exercise personally, allow time for everyone in the group to share whatever word or insight they have discovered, if they feel comfortable. This exercise can lead to very personal insights and discoveries that you may not yet feel ready to share with others.

GO IN PEACE [5 MINUTES]
Pray the Lord's Prayer together out loud.

CHAPTER 3: THE GRACE OF THE INCARNATION

OPENING TO GOD [5 MINUTES]
Begin with five minutes of silence followed by a brief prayer

inviting God to guide the conversation.

SOUL TRAINING: GAZING ON THE CHEEK-TO-CHEEK ICON [10-15 MINUTES]

If you are in a group of seven or more people, divide into small groups of three or four. Spend ten minutes discussing what the soul-training experience was like.

ENGAGING THE CHAPTER [10-15 MINUTES]

1. The author likens many people's understanding of the dual nature of Jesus (fully God, fully human) to that of Clark Kent and Superman. If you had to come up with a superhero that is most like Jesus, who would you choose? (Batman? Iron Man? Spider-Man? etc.)

2. Have you ever wondered if there could have been another way for God to save the world than to die on the cross? What questions do you have about the crucifixion? What does the cross mean to you?

3. The author writes, "When we surrender to Jesus, the one who lived in surrender to God, we enter into the kingdom of God." What is the hardest part about surrendering your life to God? Which area of your life (family, job, leisure time) is most difficult to surrender to the will of God?

ENGAGING THE WORD [10-20 MINUTES]

Lectio divina (see the directions in this group guide for chap. 1)
   This week's passage:

"Look, the virgin shall conceive and bear a son, and they shall name him Emmanuel," which means, "God is with us." (Matthew 1:23)

After you have finished this exercise personally, allow time for everyone in the group to share whatever word or insight they have discovered, if they feel comfortable. This exercise can lead to very personal insights and discoveries that you may not yet feel ready to share with others.

GO IN PEACE [5 MINUTES]
Pray the Lord's Prayer together out loud.

CHAPTER 4: GOD EMPTIED HIMSELF

OPENING TO GOD [5 MINUTES]
Begin with five minutes of silence followed by a brief prayer inviting God to guide the conversation.

SOUL TRAINING: WATCHING *THE PASSION OF THE CHRIST* [10-15 MINUTES]
If you are in a group of seven or more people, divide into small groups of three or four. Spend ten minutes discussing what the soul-training experience was like.

ENGAGING THE CHAPTER [10-15 MINUTES]
1. The author tells about speaking with a woman whose demeanor changed when she found out he was the main speaker. Have you ever met a "famous person" or a celebrity? Who, when and where? Did you find yourself acting differently around that person?

2. What feelings arise when you picture what it would be like for God to enter our universe?

3. The author writes, "for those who live with God in his kingdom, the cross becomes a way of life or, more clearly, the way *to*

life." How would describe your ability to put the needs of others ahead of your own?

ENGAGING THE WORD [10-20 MINUTES]
Lectio divina (see directions in this group guide for chap. 1)

This week's passage:

The Word became flesh and lived among us. (John 1:14)

After you have finished this exercise personally, allow time for everyone in the group to share whatever word or insight they have discovered, if they feel comfortable. This exercise can lead to very personal insights and discoveries that you may not yet feel ready to share with others.

GO IN PEACE [5 MINUTES]
Pray the Lord's Prayer together out loud.

CHAPTER 5: NO GREATER LOVE

OPENING TO GOD [5 MINUTES]
Begin with five minutes of silence followed by a brief prayer inviting God to guide the conversation.

SOUL TRAINING: GAZING ON THE *PIETA* [10-15 MINUTES]
If you are in a group of seven or more people, divide into small groups of three or four. Spend ten minutes discussing what the soul-training experience was like.

ENGAGING THE CHAPTER [10-15 MINUTES]
1. The opening story is about a surgery the author's brother underwent. What is the scariest medical moment you have had?

2. Have you ever been asked to make a great sacrifice for someone? If so, describe that experience. If not, how do you think you would react to the kind of sacrifice the author was asked to make?

3. The author confesses, "I have moments of self-sacrifice but days of self-centeredness." Do you relate to this statement? Explain.

ENGAGING THE WORD [10-20 MINUTES]
Lectio divina (see directions in this group guide for chap. 1)
This week's passage:

No one has greater love than this, to lay down one's life for one's friends. (John 15:13)

After you have finished this exercise personally, allow time for everyone in the group to share whatever word or insight they have discovered, if they feel comfortable. This exercise can lead to very personal insights and discoveries that you may not yet feel ready to share with others.

GO IN PEACE [5 MINUTES]
Pray the Lord's Prayer together out loud.

CHAPTER 6: THE DEEPER MAGIC

OPENING TO GOD [5 MINUTES]
Begin with five minutes of silence followed by a brief prayer inviting God to guide the conversation.

SOUL TRAINING: WATCHING *THE LION, THE WITCH, AND THE WARDROBE* [10-15 MINUTES]
If you are in a group of seven or more people, divide into small groups of three or four. Spend ten minutes discussing what the

soul-training experience was like.

ENGAGING THE CHAPTER [10-15 MINUTES]

1. This chapter deals with theories of the atonement or ways we try to explain what Jesus did for us on the cross. Think back to the time you first gave your life to God—what message or gospel or explanation of what God had done for you helped you make a decision to accept Jesus as Lord?

2. Which theory of the atonement did you hear the most when you were growing up? Did it influence how you thought about God?

3. The author states, "Self-sacrifice is not weakness. The courage to lay down our life for another is the greatest power this world has ever known." In what circumstance would you willingly offer your life for the sake of another?

ENGAGING THE WORD [10-20 MINUTES]

Lectio divina (see the directions in this group guide for chap. 1)
This week's passage:

"For in him all the fullness of God was pleased to dwell, and through him God was pleased to reconcile to himself all things, whether on earth or in heaven, by making peace through the blood of his cross." (Colossians 1:19-20)

After you have finished this exercise personally, allow time for everyone in the group to share whatever word or insight they have discovered, if they feel comfortable. This exercise can lead to very personal insights and discoveries that you may not yet feel ready to share with others.

GO IN PEACE [5 MINUTES]

Pray the Lord's Prayer together out loud.

Notes

Chapter 1: The Economy of the Kingdom

p. 15   icons meaningful to Nouwen's spiritual life: Henri Nouwen, *Behold the Beauty of the Lord: Praying with Icons* (Notre Dame, Ind.: Ave Maria Press, 2007).

p. 16   Rublev's depiction of the Trinity: The Ten Commandments forbid depicting God in any image. Rublev uses the angel motif to get around this problem.

Chapter 2: A God Who Seeks Our Good

pp. 20-21   "We admitted we were powerless": The first of twelve steps of Alcoholics Anonymous. See "The 12 Steps," *12Step.org* <www.12step.org/the-12-steps.html>.

Chapter 3: The Grace of the Incarnation

p. 24   "The Incarnation is to be understood as": Thomas F. Torrance, *The Mediation of Christ* (Colorado Springs: Helmers & Howard, 1992), p. 39.

p. 26   "Why did the Father will [the crucifixion]?": Edward Yarnold, "The Theology of Christian Spirituality," in *The Study of Spirituality,* ed. Cheslyn Jones, Geoffrey Wainwright and Edward Yarnold (Oxford: Oxford University Press, 1986), p. 15.

p. 28   the cheek-to-cheek icon: Called "The Korsun Mother of God," nineteenth-century Russian.

Chapter 4: God Emptied Himself

p. 34   "I am bought by the sufferings and death of Jesus": Dallas Willard, *The Divine Conspiracy* (San Francisco: HarperSanFrancisco, 1998), p. 334.

pp. 34-35   "The individual disciples must have indelibly imprinted": Ibid., p. 335.

THE
APPRENTICE
SERIES

The Good and Beautiful God

The Good and Beautiful Life

The Good and Beautiful Community

For more information and resources visit
www.apprenticeofJesus.org

God is stamping "aprentis" hearts with his kingdom purposes. He'll use *you* to change the world.

APRENTIS SERVES

Churches. Through a ministry of discipleship and formation, God can radically transform the way your church community lives and works and loves.

Like-minded leaders, organizations and thinkers. Collaborate with us to archive, engage and expand the field of Christian spiritual formation.

Students. Through an undergraduate degree track and second major in Christian spiritual formation, you can begin a serious life transformation through your college experience.

Begin an "apprentice" journey today.
For more information, contact the Aprentis Institute
at 316.295.5519 or email Aprentis@friends.edu.

APRENTIS
Institute for Christian Spiritual Formation

FRIENDS
UNIVERSITY

RENOVARÉ
www.renovare.org

Just over twenty years ago Richard J. Foster, my mentor and friend, said to me, "Jim, I'm starting a ministry. It is time for the walls to come down that separate denominations. The church needs to do better at its primary job—making disciples. And people need to learn how to practice the disciplines not just as individuals but within groups. We need to help the modern church connect to the ancient church. I'd like you to help me design it and help lead it." I said yes. A month later we met for lunch and Richard told me he had come up with a name for this spiritual renewal ministry: RENOVARÉ (ren-o-var-ay), a Latin word that means "to renew." I knew right away we were in trouble: no one could pronounce it, and no one knew what it meant. But it sounded really cool, because from the very start it was already doing what nobody else dared to.

Most parachurch organizations set out to do what they think churches aren't doing on their own, but RENOVARÉ comes alongside churches and resources them without pretending to do their job, namely, making disciples of Jesus Christ. Unfortunately, people have separated the word *disciple* from discipline. They forget that the followers of Christ were *disciples* because they practiced the *disciplines* of Christ, and the disciples' spiritual lives were made rich through the practices of prayer, morality, sharing the gospel, service, Communion and spiritual gifts.

RENOVARÉ is helping us—individuals and churches—to overcome our forgetfulness and rediscover these practices, these disciplines, in order that we, like the first-century Christians, can know what it is to walk closely with Jesus and become more like him. I've worked with RENOVARÉ for all these years (and partnered with them in the development of this book series) because they know that following Christ goes beyond denominations, even beyond the latest church program, and gives us tools to discovering life with God in the very fabric of our everyday lives.

This book is very much a part of what RENOVARÉ is all about—it has the same DNA as RENOVARÉ. So I hope you don't stop here, because as an organization and a community of the most kind and Christlike people I know, RENOVARÉ continues the conversation and the journey you have begun in this book. Come and walk with us.